695
8/07

D1361211

ART NOUVEAU
GLASS AND CERAMICS

ART NOUVEAU
GLASS AND CERAMICS

Grange BOOKS

A QUANTUM BOOK

Published by Grange Books
an imprint of Grange Books Plc
The Grange
Kingsnorth Industrial Estate
Hoo, nr. Rochester
Kent ME3 9ND

1-84013-124-1

This book is produced by
Quantum Books Ltd
6 Blundell Street
London N7 9BH

Project Manager: Rebecca Kingsley
Project Editor: Judith Millidge
Designer: Wayne Humphries
Editor: Clare Haworth-Maden

The material in this publication previously appeared in
*Encyclopedia of Decorative Arts, Illustrated History of
Antiques, A Guide to Art Nouveau Style, Introduction to the
Decorative Arts, Art of Louis Comfort Tiffany, Art of Rene
Lalique*

QUMANGC
Set in Times
Reproduced in Singapore by Eray Scan Pte Ltd
Printed in Singapore by Star Standard Industries (Pte) Ltd

42310238

CONTENTS

INTRODUCTION

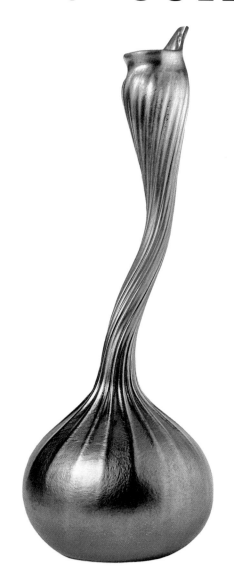

Art Nouveau glass and ceramics were closely linked in both style and technique and much the same kind of ware was produced in each medium. In both crafts, the innovations of Art Nouveau increased the range of colour and the possibilities for relief decoration, as well as changing the actual shape of the piece itself. For the Art Nouveau craftsman, glass and clay were, in their own way, as malleable and tractable as metal, and the fluid contours of the style could be equally well expressed.

Far left: A goose-necked vase by Louis Comfort Tiffany, inspired by a Persian perfume flask.

THE STYLES OF THE CENTURY

Art Nouveau developed in the late 1880s and was at its creative height in the subsequent decade. By 1905 it had declined into being a much diluted ingredient in commercial design,

soon to be replaced by an aesthetic felt to be more in keeping with the new century.

The 19th century had seen enormous changes in society in both Europe and America, with the spread of industrialisation

Below: New machinery at the 1851 Great Exhibition, London, which had introduced the mass production of everyday artefacts and threatend the role of craftsmen.

7

resulting in great wealth mainly concentrated in the new manufacturing and commercial cities. Mass production methods in factories not only produced a wider range of goods that were more widely available than ever before, but also created an entirely new class of workers. At the same time, major advances in technology such as railways, steamships and the telegraph, were easing the problems of communication. The world had changed, yet it seemeded as though there were no corresponding changes in the styles employed to shape its appearance. In the design of everyday objects, just as in the design of buildings, the new age was simply offering revivals of old styles: Classical, Gothic, Renaissance, Baroque or Rococo. While technology advanced, the quality of design seemed to have stagnated or even regressed.

NEW ART

The Art Nouveau – the 'new art' – was the first style that did not seem to have its roots sunk deep into European history. Art Nouveau was the first new style of the 19th century – despite the fact that it did not emerge until its closing years.

ART AND INDUSTRY

The Art Nouveau style was made possible by a number of outstanding writers on aesthetics during the 19th century, notably John Ruskin and William Morris in Britain, and Léon de Laborde and Eugène Viollet-le-Duc in France. What all these writers had in common was a rejection of the crass materialism which had reached its peak in many of the exhibits that were on display at the 1851 Great Exhibition

Left: Three 'Historical Revival' Goblets from Germany, c..1890.

at the Crystal Palace in London's Hyde Park. The long-forgotten truth that art should be in harmony with the age which produces it was rediscovered around 1850 by these men.

John Ruskin was especially responsible for a number of advances in the field of aesthetics: he rejected the distinction between the so-called major and minor arts. Consequently, interior decoration, which had formerly been entirely in the hands of artisans, now took on the dimensions of a major social and artistic mission to be accomplished. According to Ruskin, the decorative arts should once again assume the central position in artistic concerns they had occupied at the time of the Renaissance.

INSPIRATION FROM NATURE
It was also Ruskin who called upon architects to draw their inspiration from nature. This concept was to be central to the movements in the decorative arts at the end of the nineteenth century. The translation of the 'secrets' of nature into design are evident in the works of Art Nouveau architects like Victor Horta in Belgium and Hector Guimard in Paris, in the glass of Gallé, the Daum Brothers, Lalique and Tiffany, and in the ceramics of Chaplet, Carriers and Delahérches.

Count Léon de Laborde had been in charge of organising the French participation at the 1851 Great Exhibition and although many of the 1,756 French exhibitors won awards, Laborde was not uncritical of their works. Unlike many of his contemporaries, he did not make a cult of the past and he was against artists who killed art by making a fetish of copying the masterpieces of past ages. At the

Right: Sevres 'De Monteforte' vase, c.1908, a fine example of the Art Nouveau style.

Above: In his own house and studio, Victor Horta's adventurous use of ironwork is demonstrated in the elaborate baclonies.

Right: Portrait of John Ruskin by T.B Wirgman.

beginning of his report published in 1856, Laborde made a revolutionary statement: 'The future of the Arts, of the Sciences and of Industry lies in their association.'

TRANSPLANTATION

Eugène Viollet-le-Duc, in his *Entretiens sur l'Architecture*, suggested that it was barbarous to reproduce a Greek temple in London or Paris, since such a 'transplantation' revealed an ignorance of the basic principles which governed its construction. He wrote further that interior decoration had lost its unity because the architect was not concerned with the paintings that would be hung in the rooms he had designed, the painter never took account of the rooms in which his work would be placed, the furniture maker completely ignored both the architect and the painter, and the man who made the curtains was only concerned that his work was all that was noticed anyway!

Through their writings, Ruskin, Laborde and Viollet-le-Duc were to have a determining influence on the formation of the new modern style for which they had pleaded. Although they often contradicted themselves, they did at least try to resolve the dichotomy between Art and Industry which was the major problem of their age.

REFORM IN DESIGN

To Ruskin, it seemed that the machine was at the root of the problem of design. Ruskin abhorred the products of mass-production and called for a return to craftsmanship inspired by a romantic view of the Middle Ages. By revitalising the crafts, Ruskin hoped to develop an alternative to what he saw as the horrors of factory labour, as well as improving the aesthetic quality of everyday objects.

MORRIS AND CRAFTSMANSHIP

Ruskin's ideas were taken up by his disciple William Morris, the craftsman, poet, printer, textile and graphic designer and sometime painter. Morris began his career, firstly as a painter as a follower of the group of Pre-Raphaelite artists. As a student at Oxford, Morris had met and become friends with the painter Edward Burne-Jones, the painter and poet Dante Gabriel Rossetti and architect Philip Webb. All shared Morris's enthusiasm for the culture of the Middle Ages and were inspired not only by its architecture, art and crafts, but by the spirit of artistic co-operation which had fostered their creation.

PRACTICAL VICTORIANS

Morris, however, had a practical Victorian view of the period when he came to recreate an idyll of painters, architects and craftsmen working together on the same tasks. In 1861, he founded a company to produce the type of objects he wanted to see in every home, which became Morris & Co. Morris was able to bridge the divide between artists and craftsmen by employing his own friends to design and dec-

Above: A vaulted hall from Viollet-le-Duc's Entretiens sur l'Architecture.

Right: William Morris in 1877 when the Arts and Crafts Movement that he had created was beginning to revolutionise English design.

orate furniture, create tapestries, fabrics, printed books and wallpapers. In so doing, Morris was able to produce a complete range of goods to furnish the home that were in a uniform style and created an overall harmony of effect. In this, and in his insistence that it was the observation of nature and its forms that was the basis for all design, Morris anticipated the versatility of the Art Nouveau artist-craftsman.

HIGH IDEALS
Throughout his career, Morris struggled to reconcile his high artistic ideals with his social and political inclinations. His commitment to the creation of products that reflected the highest standards of design and construction were constantly at odds with his desire to produce them at a cost that consumers could

reasonably afford. His dedication to the principles of handcrafting conflicted with the need for machine production which could reduce the drudgery of certain tasks and reduce production costs. The successful marriage of art and industry was a dilemma that he was never to fully resolve. Nevertheless, his example encouraged many similar enterprises in Britain and overseas, usually referred to under the general term 'Arts and Crafts Movement'.

MACKMURDO AND THE CENTURY GUILD
Chief among the Arts and Crafts Movement groups was the Century Guild, formed in 1884 by Arthur Heygate Mackmurdo. Influenced by the flowing natural forms used by Morris, Mackmurdo developed these further into more elongated, sinuous and increasingly elegant patterns. In his illustration to the title page of *Wren's City Churches*, where the stems of the flowers undulate in an asymmetrical, rippling pattern like marine plants gently animated by unseen currents, Mackmurdo created the sinuous shapes and lines that were to become the hallmark of Art Nouveau for the next 20 years.

THE CRAFTS REVITALISED
As with the other crafts revitalised by Morris and his followers, the histories of glassware and ceramics of the 19th century were the stories of technical advances which resulted in an impressively consistent quality of mechanical production. However, this was achieved largely at the expense of aesthetic distinction.

To the Arts and Crafts Movement glass meant, above all else, the stained glass of their neo-medieval church windows. It was not until the 1890s, when Christopher Dresser began designing for the Clutha range of James Couper & Sons of Glasgow, that distinguished con-

Left: The Orchard Tapestry, designed by Morris and woven at Merton in 1890 for Jesus College Chapel, Cambridge, is an example of Morris's use of high warp, or vertical, tapestry technique.

Above : Morris & Co painted glass from Wightwick Manor. The figure of Chaucer emphasises the medieval inspiration for Arts and Crafts glass.

Right: William de Morgan was associated with Morris, and in 1872 founded his own pottery and showroom in Chelsea, London.

Far right: Earthenware vase and cover by William de Morgan painted with a brightly coloured floral and foliate design, inspired by Iznik pottery of Persia.

temporary glassware was to be seen in Britain with an Art Nouveau sense of line and colour. In ceramics, the reaction against industrialisation occurred a little earlier. In France, Théodore Deck, who set up his workshop in Paris in 1856, can be considered as the first of the 'art-potter' craftsmen. Deck was inspired principally by Near-Eastern and Persian designs and experimented with high-temperature glazes and oriental shapes and designs.

In England, this was echoed by W. Howson Taylor at his Ruskin Pottery near Birmingham, and by Bernard Moore in Staffordshire, but the first true art-potter, and the one most closely attuned to Morris's principles was William de Morgan, who produced earthenware pieces in lustre, and bright, Persian designs from the 1870s.

ART NOUVEAU EMERGES

When he chose it as the name for the shop, La Maison de l'Art Nouveau, which he opened in 1895, Samuel Bing did not invent the expression 'Art Nouveau'. In fact, the term had been around since 1884 when the two Belgians, Octave Maus and Edmond Picard, who had created the review *L'Art Moderne,* proclaimed themselves as 'believers in Art Nouveau', an art which refused to accept the prevailing cult of the past. At first, the term was attached to the works of painters who rejected academicism. The more specialised use of the term Art Nouveau, for architecture and art objects, was to come later. At the same time different countries were to create their own specific versions of the term: Jugendstil, Sezessionstill, Modern Style, Stile Liberty, Modernismo or even Belgische Stil.

Despite the different names, each movement has a number of common features. Firstly, there was the rejection of academic traditions. For anyone wishing to create Art Nouveau, the cult of antiquity was a thing of the past. The rejection of antiquity went hand in hand with a return to the observation and imitation of nature. The straight line was abandoned in favour of the curve, the essence of Art Nouveau. The characteristic curving forms of Art Nouveau which first appeared in England were to spread rapidly throughout Europe and America to a range of centres each with their own distinctive interpretations of the style.

THE NEW ART IN FULL FLOWER

While the 1890s saw the development of Art Nouveau, the fully evolved characteristics of the style which enjoyed their greatest success were to be seen at the 1900 Paris Universal Exhibition. It was here that the concept of Art Nouveau design as a 'total' one emerged.

Above: 'Rose de France' glass vase by Emile Galle, c.1900.

Left: Otto Eckmann's cover for the journal, Jugend.

Designers were seen as 'ensembliers', rather than as creators of individual pieces. In truth, Art Nouveau could only be seen at its best in a complete ensemble, something, once again, that only a limited number of patrons desired or could afford. As manufacturers quick to cash in on the popularity of the style attempted synthetic versions for mass production, Art Nouveau was inevitably to deteriorate.

EUROPEAN
ART NOUVEAU
GLASS

As with other crafts revitalised by the Art Nouveau, the history of glassware in the earlier part of the nineteenth century, was the story of technical advances, resulting in an impressively consistent quality of mechanical production. The technique of press moulding was invented in the United States in the 1820s and steam power was applied to the process of glass cutting. More important was an accelerating interest in the chemical compositions of glass recipes and moves to increase the efficiency of firing. Stylistically, until Art Nouveau emerged at the end of the century, glass in the 19th century was once again marked by eclecticism and stylistic revivalism.

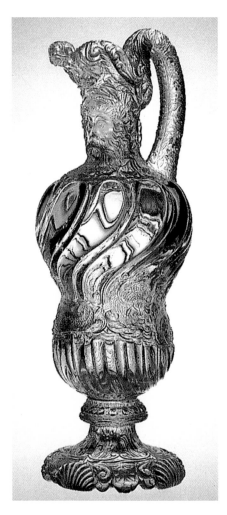

Above: Rock crystal ewer made in Stourbridge in 1886. The elaborate aquatic motifs were engraved by William Fritsche.

Overleaf:Art Nouveau stained glass. Sinuous lines end in a whiplash.

ART NOUVEAU GLASS IN FRANCE

By the 1890s, French luxury glass production had reached a remarkably high standard of technical and creative inspiration. This major achievement can be traced back to a small, but significant number of talented artists, notably, Philippe-Joseph Brocard, Auguste Jean and Eugène Rousseau and his friend and collaborator, Ernest Léveillé.

Rousseau began his career as an art dealer before starting up as a craftsman himself. In 1878, the year that Gallé unveiled his 'clair de lune' glass with its delicate sapphire tinge, Rousseau created an equivalent sensation with his glass that imitated agates, jades and other semiprecious stones, which were sometimes enhanced by internal craquelé effects. Jean showed enamelled pieces, but his most notable innovation was in his free-form applications of glass, and in his vases of free-blown organic forms.

Above all however, it was the genius of Emile Gallé who inspired an entire generation and made the Paris Universal Exhibition of 1900 a wonderful showcase for creations in glass of unprecedented technical and artistic virtuosity.

EMILE GALLÉ

Although it produced furniture, ceramics, textiles and metalwork, the Nancy School with Gallé as its chief designer, mainly based its reputation on the production of Art Nouveau glassware. Glass was in fact the traditional industry of the city and Gallé had inherited his father's workshops in 1874. In addition to an extensive education which included botany and literature, Gallé also had a technical apprenticeship in glassworks at the Meisenthal glassworks (now in Germany). The inspiration for Gallé's own work was rich and varied. As with so many of the avant-garde of his generation, an introduction to Japanese art helped him to create a new visual language. His ability to create elegant, almost abstract graphic designs from the plant and insect life that were his most constant source of motifs owes a debt to Oriental art. The motto over his studio door however, 'My roots are deep in the woods' demonstrated that his greatest source of inspiration was nature.

Gallé's more personal creations also reflect his literary interests; he often used the works of contemporary French poets directly on his glass. His *verreries parlantes* (talking glass-

Right: Emile Gallé in 1889.

Far right: A brush holder that is also an early example of Gallé's verreriess parlantes.

ware) were inscribed with extracts from the verses which had inspired their decoration, verses from Hugo, Baudelaire, Mallarmé, Verlaine, Gautier and Rimbaud, as well as other sources as diverse as Shakespeare and the Bible.

GOLD MEDAL

Gallé's great success came in 1889, when he won a gold medal and the Grand Prix at the Paris Exhibition. His major innovation of this time was his cameo glass, whereby glass of two or more layers was carved or etched back, leaving the design in relief in one or more colours, against a contrasting ground. The technique was copied from that of Chinese Chien Lung cased glass that Gallé had studied in the South Kensington Museum in London. It was on a mass-produced, acid-etched version of his cameo technique that Gallé was to base the prosperity of his business. The combined effects of colour and translucence provided Gallé with the marvellous colour effects which suggested submarine creatures against drifting seaweed, beetles crawling through long grass, or a butterfly settling on a flower.

1897 saw him introduce another new technique, *marqueterie-sur-verre*, which involved inlaying semi-molten glass details of decoration into the semi-molten body of the piece being worked on. A combination of several different ingredients might also be used, as in the example of champleve, in which the cavities created in the glass were lined with gilt, before being filled in with layers of translucent enamels whose glow would be enhanced by the gold backing.

The 1900 Paris Universal Exhibition was perhaps the finest hour for Art Nouveau glass, it was also to be Gallé's last major showing before his death in 1904. By the turn of the century Gallé was showing more sculptural

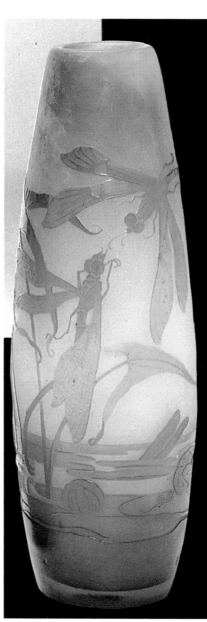

freedom, producing pieces of completely organic form, or worked in high relief with fluid applications of glass. Two of his greatest masterpieces, the *Main aux Algues,* and the extraordinary and beautiful lamp, *Les Coprins*, date from this later period.

FUNCTIONAL DESIGN

In the best tradition of Art Nouveau, Gallé's glassware was prized far more as an artistic creation than for its functional design, and as such was collected by aesthetes and writers. His reputation rested upon a limited production of works which required an enormous number of man hours. A growing demand for his works encouraged him to increase capacity, but the more numerous workshop designs inevitably lacked the degree of finish of his earlier works. Nevertheless, Gallé's influence on contemporary glass makers was considerable, and he led a great renaissance of the industry in Nancy.

THE NANCY SCHOOL

In 1901 a group of artists allied themselves as the Ecole de Nancy, Alliance Provinciale des Industries d'Art. With Gallé as their guiding light, Louis Majorelle, Eugène Vallin and the Daum brothers were vice-presidents of the union. The Nancy School style of glass became prevalent in France produced by local firms such as the Muller brothers, the Verrerie de Nancy of the Daum brothers, and that of Auguste Legras who had taken over the Cristaleries of Saint Denis and of Pantin.

THE DAUM BROTHERS

Although Legras was operating the largest glassworks, employing some 1,500 people, the most notable rivals to Emile Gallé were the Daum brothers, Auguste and Antonin, who

Right: Gallé's cameo glass, where two or more layers of glass were fused together and engraved.

were also more dependent than Gallé on the creativity of their employees. Nevertheless, the Daums tuned this to their advantage as they counted among their contributors Jacques Gruber (who later turned his interest to furniture making), Eugène Goll (their most talented glass worker who was responsible for some of the most sculptural and inventive pieces), and Alméric Walter, who developed the *pâte-de-verre* technique for the company.

ACID ETCHING
The Daum brothers were, like Gallé, concerned with opacity, colour and relief, and used acid to etch away layers of glass to reveal the colours beneath and create delicately modulated backgrounds for relief work. To produce a glowing, opaque finish in a variety of colours, powdered enamels were fused onto the surfaces of pieces during firing.

PÊTE-DE-VERRE
The Daum brothers were also involved in the development of glassware produced by a more lengthy process in which pre-manufactured, ground-down glass was used as an ingredient. By manipulating the oxidation process, an opaque glass known as *pâte-de-verre*, could be produced which had a similar appearance to alabaster. The technique of *pâte-de-verre* was first revived in the 19th century by artist-sculptor Henri Cros as a sort of mock marble. Cros made reliefs and free standing sculptures on a small scale and largely based on classical themes. The Daum brothers were the first to exploit the rediscovery on a commercial scale and produced designs by Alméric Walter, but the greatest exponent of the technique was François-Emile Décorchemont. His earliest pieces had thin bodies with trailing

Above: Glass vase by Emile Gallé with decoration in marquetry-sur-verre, c.1900.

Left: Gallé vase with marquetry-sur-verre on a translucent base engraved with irises.

Right: Les Coprins lamp, c.1900 by Emile Gallé illustrates three stages of growth in a mushroom.

Art Nouveau motifs such as seaweed and other natural forms.

RENÉ LALIQUE

The great maestro René Lalique's interest in glass also dated to the 1890s when he began using cast glass in multi-media works of art. Around 1900 he began to use glass in his exquisite jewellery, caring little for the lack of intrinsic value of glass if its qualities were appropriate to the design. Around this time, Lalique began experimenting with the creation of all glass *cire perdue* pieces, including vases and panels such as the ones he used as decorations in his own home.

In 1902 Lalique set up a small glassworks and his first commercial commission was from the parfumeur, François Coty, who approached him to design scent bottles. Concentrating on large scale production, by 1912 Lalique's career as a jeweller was over and a new career in glassware design opened. Until the final close of production in 1939, the firm of Verrerie d'Art-René Lalique & Cie., at Wingen-sur-Moder produced an extensive range of vases, glasses and other tableware, as well as scent bottles and the famous motor car mascots. Lalique's greatest distinction was not for any remarkable quality of work, but the stylish repertoire of designs ranging from elegant evocations of the Art Nouveau age through the modern motifs of Art Deco. Combining modern techniques of mass production with a high level of artistic involvement, Lalique raised glasswork to the level of fine art in an idiom as appropriate to the 20th century as that of Gallé had been to the fin-de-siècle.

ART NOUVEAU GLASS IN BRITAIN

In England, while William Morris and his followers had sought to redress the imbalance between mechanical production and the poor quality of contemporary design by reviving traditional crafts, to a large extent, glassware did not benefit from the same outpouring of interest.

STAINED GLASS WINDOWS

To the Arts and Crafts Movement, glass meant stained glass windows, and within the movement the two most famous makers of decorative glass were the firms of Powell's of Whitefriars, and James Couper & Sons of Glasgow. From 1890 to 1900, Powell's had pioneered forms of glass which relied more on firing techniques and upon the form itself rather than the decoration. The firm had earlier produced stained glass for Morris & Co. and simple, uncut table glass for the architect Philip Webb, and were happy to absorb the Arts and Crafts principles of beauty lying in shape and method of production rather than applied decoration.

CLUTHA GLASS

Truly distinguished glassware was developed by Christopher Dresser for Couper & Sons in the mid-1890s when the firm produced a range called Clutha glass. Freed by the nature of glass from an adherence to strict principles of utility, Dresser's forms are irregular, following the sinuousness and rhythms of organic growth that is the central motif of Art Nouveau.

The blown Clutha glass uses opaque green glass, often shot with translucent streaks of gold or cream, and was the result of Dresser's interest in ancient Roman and Middle Eastern glass. Similar Art Nouveau forms were also used by the firm of Stuart & Sons of Stourbridge, which specialised in furnace decoration, and Stevens & Williams, also of

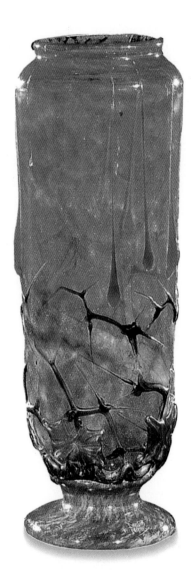

Above: The Daum Brothers' glass is clearly influenced by Gallé.

Above: The Daums achieved a consistently high standard, decorating their surfaces with a charming, light touch.

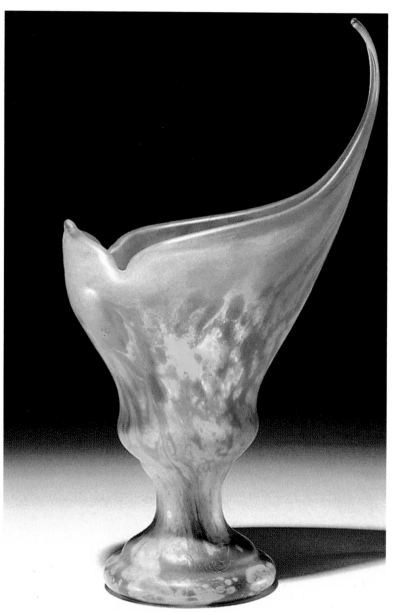

Stourbridge who experimented with crackled glass and silver deposit decoration.

ART NOUVEAU GLASS IN GERMANY AND AUSTRIA

If the great names of Art Nouveau glass in France and America are Gallé and Tiffany, in Austria the greatest of the Art Nouveau glass makers was the Loetz factory. Surprisingly, Loetz glass is the least highly valued today in terms of the art market largely because the glass remains 'anonymous': it relates not to a named, individual or personality but to a corporate image.

THE LOETZ FACTORY

The Loetz factory was founded at Klostermühle in 1836. In 1879 Max von Spaun became head of the factory and for the next eleven years he oversaw the production of seven varieties of decorative glass, many of which attempted to imitate the surface appearance of different types of hardstones. The firm produced its first iridescent pieces in the 1880s and in 1898 at the Vienna Jubilee Exhibition, Loetz showed a major group of iridescent glass. In addition to the designs by von Spaun himself, Loetz also commissioned designs from Joseph Hoffmann, Kolomon Moser, Otto Prutscher, Dagobert Peche and Michael Powlony. The members of the Wiener Werkstätte were involved as designers with most of the leading Austro-Hungarian glass houses at this time, as they were with most of the potteries and in this period, Loetz executed pieces on commission from members of the Werkstätte.

Two other prestigious firms in Austria, J & L Lobmeyr and Graf Harrach, were located in Vienna. Lobmeyr produced high-quality

Left: Daum Brothers' glass chalice.

table glass but they also marketed decorative items including engraved and etched work on enamelled pieces in a rather Middle-Eastern style. The company also produced pieces designed by the members of the Werstatte and Joseph Hoffmann designed what is probably his best known range of decorated glass for Lobmeyr. These pieces of clear or matt glass were decorated with opaque black or grey motifs in a type of decoration known as 'bronzidecor'.

HARRACH GLASS HOUSE
In 1898 at the Vienna Jubilee Exhibition, the Harrach glass house showed glass that was obviously in imitation of the great American glass maker, Louis Comfort Tiffany. But, by 1900 the company had widened its scope to include cameo glass in the style of Gallé and enamelled pieces decorated with designs inspired by Alphonse Mucha.

Below: Owls Bracelet by René Lalique, c.1900-01 in gold, glass, chalcedony and enamel.

GERMAN GLASS
In Germany there were a number of important Art Nouveau designers, the most significant of whom was Karl Koepping. He had trained as a painter and etcher in Munich but began experimenting in glass around 1895. To execute his designs, Koepping hired an expert glass blower Friedrich Zitmann but after a disagreement in 1896, Koepping's pieces were made by the impressively named, Grossherzogliche Sachlische Fachshule und Lehrwerkstätte fur Glasinstrumentmacher und Mechaniker. Koepping's tall, spindly pieces with extraordinary curving stems, were greatly admired and were sold by Bing in Paris at La Maison de l'Art Nouveau. Zitmann continued his own glass-making enterprise, and around 1897 began making iridescent glass with bubbling and pitting which imitated the amazing surface effects of recently excavated ancient Roman glass. Glass of this type

Right: A Lalique 'Styx' flacon for Coty, 1910-13.

15

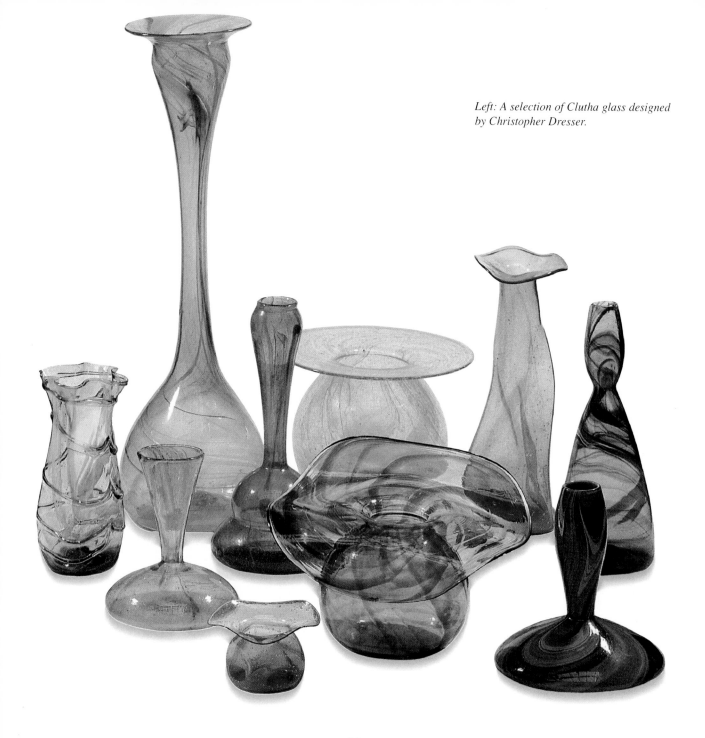

was also to be the inspiration for Tiffany's Cypriote glass which he first made around 1895-96.

The German Secessionist involvement in glass was not as influential or as widespread as in Austria. The WMF glass factory, established in 1881, principally made glass liners for its metalwork. In 1883 it did establish a serious glass concern but did not produce art glass until the 1920s when they marketed iridescent pieces called Ikora-Kristall and Myra-Krystall.

A NEW CHALLENGE

The invention of the incandescent electric lamp by Thomas Edison in the 1880s gave a new challenge to glass designers, who were no longer bound by the need to create lamps that could shield users from a flame. Louis Comfort Tiffany was among the first to recognise the potential of electricity for the Art Nouveau style and his name was to become synonymous with the style of lamp which used coloured glass set into leaded panels rather like a stained glass window.

Above: Austrian Art Nouveau glassware by (left to right) Zasche, Powlony and von Harrach.

MIXED MEDIA

The opportunity for mixed media work in glass, metal and ceramics was to give the electric lamp an instant appeal for Art Nouveau,, quite apart from the bright, even light that it could harness as part of the overall composition. It is a typical tendency of Art Nouveau that the modernity of the electric light, with its startlingly technological aspect heralding the dawn of a new age, was to be ignored by many designers. Instead, filtered by coloured glass, the electric light became a gentle glow, a part of the fantastic idylls of decorative lilies, swans and butterflies that kept the Art Nouveau interior separate from, and unsullied by, brutish technology.

The treatment of the electric lamp in the hands of the masters like Gallé or Tiffany parallels the use of wrought iron in architecture by Horta or Guimard. It is used willingly, but, although playing a major part in the whole, it is masked by its conversion, against its very manufactured nature, into the organic world of Art Nouveau.

Both Gallé and the Daum brothers produced lamps in a style very similar to their other glassware. Glass figured as both base, neck and shade, and, typically, the form of the mushroom was used as the most analogous form in nature. While other table, bracket and standing lamps did use more metalwork, the plant form naturally remained part of the design.

METAL PLANTS

In works by Louis Majorelle, Hector Guimard, Eugène Vallin and Emile Gallé, sinuous metal plants or tree saplings are created which flower

Left: A Daum Brothers' night-light. The combination of glassware and electric light was irresistible to Art Nouveau designers.

into electric bulbs. These were used in the same way in which an Art Nouveau designer set a precious stone in a piece of jewellery: the whole setting, whether a vine, a tree or a flower, constitutes the bulk of the work, while the light bulbs are scattered around the metalwork as highlights.

LAMPS

While many Art Nouveau lamps feature glowing flowers, the bronze or gilt statuettes of nymph-like figures that were produced by many craftsmen could also be adapted to carry an electric light. In so doing, these pieces provide an interplay between function and ornamentation. The lightly-draped female figures which supported desk lamps are perhaps, an indication of Art Nouveau's retreat from the challenge of the new medium, for they have an escapist charm. To the next generation of designers, they revealed only a retreat into the impractical fantasies at odds with the nature of the artefact itself. From the wide range of Art Nouveau craftsmen and designers, only the Belgian Henry Van de Velde, commissioned by Bing, produced an electric lamp that took as its starting point the functional, practical and scientific nature of the medium.

ARCHITECTURAL GLASS

If the 1900 Paris Universal Exhibition marked the high point for luxury and elaborately wrought glass into works of art, it was also the occasion for a prediction by Eugène Houtart that 'Steel and glass are without doubt the two elements which will characterise the twentieth century and will give their name to it.' After the First World War, Houtart's prediction seemed to find its fulfilment when glass became the chosen material for designs of every scale, from the mass production of

Below: Tiffany lamp with a poppy motif glass shade from around 1900.

Right: A window by Georges de Feure. The elegant and alluring female is derived from the work of Aubrey Beardsley and relates strongly to de Feure's graphic work.

Lalique's perfume bottle, to the glass curtain-walled architecture of the Modernists.

At the end of the 19th century, however, a more traditional part of glass design was that of stained glass. A huge revival of interest in its design and manufacture had accompanied the Gothic revival and it continued to be an important art form with the medievally-inspired English Arts and Crafts Movement.

MORRIS & CO.

In its early years, the firm of Morris & Co. had depended financially on their stained glass. Dante Gabriel Rossetti, Henry Holiday and William Morris had all designed stained glass to meet the ecclesiastical demand created by the Gothic revival, but the firms' most notable designer was the painter Edward Burne-Jones who adopted a free flowing style in both lead lines and painting with strong, vibrant colours and naturalistic form.

INFLUENCES

The Art Nouveau treatment of stained glass grew from this revival, and profited by the growing decorative similarities between stained glass, embroideries and paintings. The first two crafts, by their very nature, were concerned with two-dimensionality, and, took their cue from the crafts, painters and graphic designers of the 1890s such as Paul Gauguin, Toulouse-Lautrec, Aubrey Beardsley, Alphonse Mucha, Will Bradley and Gustav Klimt were also exploring the flat decorative arrangement of colour in their work.

For the Art Nouveau designer then, stained glass was not so much a revivalist anachronism, but a medium that was perfectly suited to the flatness, linearity and love of light and colour that were common to all the contemporary decorative arts. As an ensemblier, the

Art Nouveau designer often wanted to control the quality and strength of the light cast on his interiors by making it harmonise with the flowing plant forms of the furniture, wallpaper and table ornaments. Tiffany even believed that stained glass in architecture played an important social role. In an age when city dwellers were often looking out onto a bare wall, a stained glass window could shield the owner from such a brutal sight and provide him with an idyllic Art Nouveau world of flowers, butterflies and birds to gaze upon instead.

Widely manufactured, stained glass was evident to some degree in almost every well-to-do home of the period. Yet most Art Nouveau stained glass did not represent the highest levels of craftsmanship, but rather, regularly shaped, painted or enamelled panes that were easy to produce and assemble. Only in the finest quality designs was the traditional method of production retained in which each motif was carefully outlined in lead, using panels of different shapes and sizes. In Nancy, Jacques Gruber produced his stained glass in this way as did Hector Guimard in Paris.

For many of the Art Nouveau architects, glass was designed as part of an architectural whole. Charles Rennie Mackintosh's designs for Miss Cranston's Willow Tea Rooms in Sauchiehall Street, Glasgow featured five tea salons, a dining gallery and a billiard room. All were decorated with a willow-leaf motif and abstracted forms related to tree shapes. The Room de Luxe was painted white with a dado, above which on three sides, was a mural made of mirror glass panels. The doors and windows were of leaded glass with the dom-

Right: The Angel Musician stained glass window designed by Edward Burne-Jones.

inant colours of purple and rose and a chandelier made of glass bubbles.

HECTOR GUIMARD

In Paris, one sees in Hector Guimard's stained glass the same abstract arches, bows and ripples evident in his ironwork. The Swiss typographer Eugène Grasset, who was also based in Paris, produced stained glass designs, too. His, however, were more traditional in subject matter than Guimard's and were strongly related to his and other's contemporary graphic art, with Art Nouveau maidens idling in summer landscapes.

Left: A window at the medical school in Nancy, France, designed by Jacques Gruber.

ART NOUVEAU GLASS
IN AMERICA

T owards the end of the 19th century, many contacts were made across the Atlantic in the field of the decorative arts. In 1876 Christopher Dresser gave a series of lectures in Philadelphia; in 1882 Oscar Wilde arrived preaching not only aesthetic ideals, but also that America should find the inspiration for her art in her own lands and not copy the styles of the past from dissimilar countries – a healthy attitude for a relatively young country. In 1893 Samuel Bing, the founder of La Maison de l'Art Nouveau, the showcase for the new style in France, visited America. In 1896 C.R Ashbee made his first visit and in 1901 met with Frank Lloyd Wright.

Above: Louis Comfort Tiffany in his middle years.

Overleaf: The John Harvard Memorial Window by John La Farge in St John's Chapel, Southwark Cathedral, London.

The flow of ideas was not only one-way, however. In the same year that Wilde toured America, the Boston architect Henry H. Richardson visited England and met William Morris and Burne-Jones. In 1889 an exhibition of American arts, including Rookwood faience ceramics and designs by John La Farge, was held in London.

GLASS IN AMERICA

While the middle of the 19th century in England had seen a considerable revival in the art of stained glass, America had not had a Gothic revival that brought with it a re-emergence of ecclesiastical art. Consequently, in America it was not until the end of the century that stained glass was seen as a promising art form.

In 1872 the illustrator and watercolourist John La Farge visited France and England where he not only admired, but met with some of the Pre-Raphaelite painters and saw the work of Morris & Co. La Farge produced his first stained glass in New York in 1876 and worked with Boston architect Henry H. Richardson and also Stanford White, who was part of the team of architects responsible for Boston Public Library.

For Richardson's Holy Trinity church in Boston, often considered the finest example of 'Richardson Romanesque', La Farge designed the panels. Around 1887 he began to experiment with different techniques which resulted in an opalescent glass which lent itself to Art Nouveau forms and no longer required painting or etching for its effects.

THE UNDOUBTED LEADER: TIFFANY

The undoubted leader in the medium, however, was Louis Comfort Tiffany. A true child of Art Nouveau, his designs and his sense of beauty matched exactly the ideals of his time. But Tiffany was no mere imitator of a fashionable artistic creed. Instead he was one of the most original designers of the Art Nouveau style and as such, his work set the standard for his peers.

TIFFANY

Tiffany's technical virtuosity is compelling. In his stained glass windows, the stippling of a bird's feather, the roughness of the bark of a tree and the gleam of water are all reproduced in the great pictorial windows he made, but none of these textures is drawn or marked into the glass. Tiffany used the mosaic system of the medieval craftsman, but his pieces of glass were not of pure colour. Instead they were a collage of colours – striped, mottled, patterned and spotted – and the colour variations themselves were contained within the glass. All the pieces in the designs are matched to allow the colours and textures to flow in a painterly manner, and the absence of brushstrokes allows the light to pass

Left: In this Tiffany stained glass window entitled 'Hudson River', plant forms dominate a vivid landscape

unhindered through the glass.

Tiffany worked unceasingly towards the aim of creating paintings in glass and it is in his abstract designs that he proved a master in stained glass. Before 1890 he designed stained glass windows that made perfect use of glass as an artistic medium. In his abstract work, in which the geometry of coloured glass is delineated by the black line of the lead, Tiffany conveyed perfectly the use of light and design that made glass its own medium and no longer an imitation of painting.

THE TIFFANY GLASS COMPANY

Tiffany also perceived a social need for decorative stained glass to create interiors full of light and warmth, where perhaps otherwise a window, especially in the city apartments, might have looked out only onto a brick wall.

Tiffany was the son of the founder of the legendary New York store, Tiffany & Co. He had studied painting under George Innes and had travelled extensively in Europe before he set up L.C Tiffany and the Associated Artists in 1879 with the help of Candace Wheeler. By the early 1880s they were the most successful New York decorating firm, and in 1882 were commissioned to decorate the White House. By 1885, however, the Association had come to an end and the independent firm of the Tiffany Glass Company was founded.

EARLY INFLUENCES

Louis Comfort Tiffany grew up in the shadow of the Tiffany workshops, and even as a child was privy to the techniques and methods of the craftsmen employed there. In

Far right: Toulouse-Lautrec's painting translated into glass by Tiffany.

particular, Edward C. Moore, a remarkable craftsman, designer and art connoisseur of whom Samuel Bing said 'his country should forever shrine him in grateful memory', was uniquely influential. Moore did not look to Europe for inspiration but rather to the East. He admired Persian and Islamic art with their geometric abstractions of natural forms and sumptuous intricacy of design. Later he became absorbed in Japanese art and its masterful use of metals. The first American to win a European award for his craft as a silversmith (the Gold Medal at the 1878 Paris Exposition), Moore was a great collector and amassed a significant collection of Oriental and antique glass which was to be of great interest in later years for Tiffany.

SOCIETY OF AMERICAN ARTISTS

Tiffany began his artistic career as a painter and exhibited regularly. Although he rarely sold his paintings, he was also active in promoting the works of other artists and helped to found the Society of American Artists which included George Innes and La Farge. Among his closest friends, however, was Samuel Colman a watercolour artist whose real interest lay in textiles. It was Colman who was directly responsible for moving Tiffany away from painting into the field of applied art.

THE FIRST EXPERIMENTS IN GLASS

Although he began as a painter, Tiffany's wealth allowed him to pursue other interests, and in 1875 he began his glass experiments in the Thill glass house in Brooklyn. He also travelled widely and collected antique Greek

Right: Not painted on glass, but an opaque glass mosaic that contained colour and texture within itself.

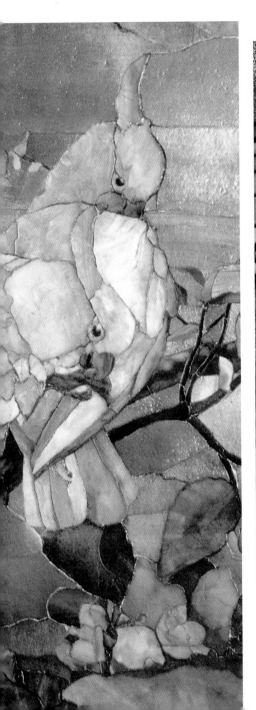

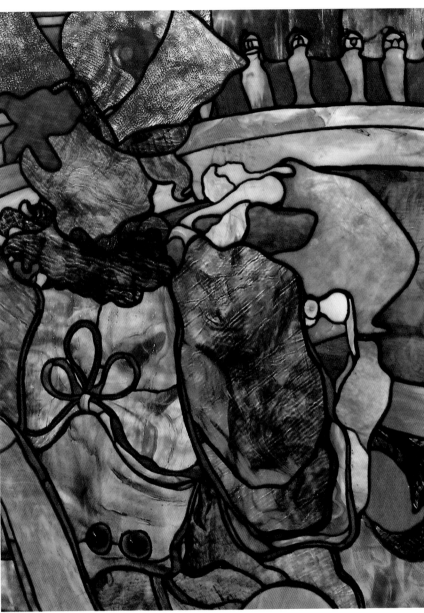

Above: A silver teaset, embellished with etching and enamels, is characteristic of the work of Edward C. Moore, the master silver smith whose taste was to influence the young L.C Tiffany.

and Roman glass, and Oriental domestic ware which represented good craftsmanship or illustrated particular working techniques. Often they carried designs from nature and thus the objects were both functional and decorative.

LOUIS C. TIFFANY AND ASSOCIATED ARTISTS

In an effort to demonstrate his own ideas regarding the unity of the arts and especially on the intermarriage of architecture and design, Tiffany invited Candace Wheeler, Samuel Colman and the collector Lockwood de Forest to join him in a design venture. The group operated under the name of 'Louis C. Tiffany and Associated Artists', and negotiated with the Society of Decorative Art for the exclusive rights to design, supervise and sell the works of its members. The overall aim was to provide 'perfect interiors' and among the many commissions they undertook were the private homes of Cornelius Vanderbilt II, the Metropolitan Museum's founder J. Taylor Johnston, the writer, Mark Twain, as well as decorating the White House. The *piece de resistance* of this scheme – unfortunately demolished in 1902 – was an opalescent glass screen that reached from floor to ceiling and which featured an intricate interlaced motif of eagles and flags.

Tiffany also continued his own work in glass and in 1878 established his own glass house. Unfortunately, this burnt down twice and it was subsequently closed down. He then began experiments at the Heidt glass house in Brooklyn and applied for a patent for a new character of glass in coloured windows. The glass tiles and lighting fixtures in many of the interiors he had designed had already attracted attention. In 1881 *Scribner's Monthly* devoted an article to glass mentioning Tiffany and La Farge as the leading exponents of the craft in America.

GLASS TILES

Towards the end of the 1880s, Tiffany began to design a great deal of mosaic work and the glass tiles were the results of his early experiments in opalescent and iridescent glass. In 1880 he made patent applications which specified three types of glass: one for use in tiles and mosaics, another for plating windows and the third to give a metallic lustre. This metallic lustre developed into his famous Favrile glass, but it is important to remember that Tiffany did not invent the iridescent lustre: in 1873 the Austrian glass makers Lobmeyr was selling iridescent glassware, and from 1878 in England Thomas Webb & Sons were producing similar glass. Tiffany never pretended to invent it, but he did believe that he made the best glass of this type.

In his early experiments Tiffany achieved many accidental effects which were quite beautiful, and later he deliberately produced irregularities of surfaces to vary and enhance the qualities of light transmission. Dissatisfied

Right: Antique Persian glassware. Tiffany envied the flowing lines, lustre and textures.

with the 'thin' colours produced by most commercial glass houses, Tiffany produced thick, dense colours ranging from ruby reds to emerald greens while abstract patterns or designs of rosettes and other plant forms were moulded onto the surface of the tiles.

TIFFANY AND ART NOUVEAU

In 1888 Tiffany undertook the commission for the decoration of the Ponce de Léon Hotel in St Augustine, Florida. The results met with high praise from the public and led to many more orders for the interior decoration department of Louis C. Tiffany and Co., the name of his company after he had parted from the Associated Artists. Many artists complained as they watched his workshops flood the market with ever more fashionable art glass windows, that Tiffany had betrayed his talent and opted for commercial success. But in 1892 Tiffany dumbfounded his critics when for Samuel Bing he executed and exhibited a stained glass window, Four Seasons. This piece was far removed from the popular designs heavy in pictorial content that Tiffany had produced in such quantities in the United States and marked the arrival of Art Nouveau in his work.

In 1889 Tiffany had visited Paris where he saw the work of the French master glass designer Emile Gallé. Gallé's engraved vases with their free-flowing shapes caught Tiffany's imagination, and in 1893 Tiffany acquired his

Right: Tiffany used glass wherever he could in his interiors. Glass tiles and stained glass dominate Mark Twain's dining room.

Far right: Tiffany's initial experiments in glass making were concentrated on glass tiles.

own glass house, the Corona furnaces on Long Island. Between this time and the end of the century, Tiffany was at his most creative and made his own unique contribution to Art Nouveau.

He turned to making what he called 'small glass' that was varied, beautiful, novel qual-ity and that expressed all the principles of Art Nouveau. Essentially organic forms abstracted into decorative surfaces and were endowed with an asymmetrical linear quality., Tiffany's favourite motifs for vases were the peacock feather, the iris, morning glories, gladioli, ten-drils and trailing leaves. But no lines were

FAVRILE

Far left: The 'Four Seasons' window. Here, 'Summer' is represented in Tiffany's masterly stained glass window.

Centre: Equally popular were Tiffany's religious subjects.

Left: Tiffany registered several trademarks. he designed two seals for his Favrile glass and in 1894 registered a logo for his the Tiffany Glass and Decorating Company.

to create different surface textures from a smooth matt to a burnished glow. Tiffany's glass rarely had the modelled plasticity of Gallé or Daum. Its decoration, far more abstract in its depiction of natural forms, rarely rises out in relief, but appears as more of an applied surface pattern.

FAVRILE GLASS

Favrile glass is a generic name: it can be divided into categories based on the various techniques used to make it. Types include Agate Ware, a thick glass which resembled marble; Lava Glass, a dark opalescent glass which had basalt or talc added to the molten glass and the surface then gold-lustred; Cypriote Glass, where the hot yellow glass of the object was covered with pulverised crumbs of the same material and then lustred. Paperweight or Reactive Glass is the term that is applied to all of Tiffany's translucent glass that had changed colour and become iridescent when it was reheated in the furnace. This was Tiffany's most technically complicated glass and no other glass maker has ever sought to imitate it.

In addition to these, Tiffany also made another type Favrile glass called Cameo Glass. It was the only type of Tiffany glass decora-

drawn or painted onto the vases, instead the molten glass was blown with small amounts of coloured glass of different textures and colours were combined and manipulated to form the decoration.

FAVRILE GLASS

In 1894 Tiffany registered Favrile as a trademark. The name is derived from the Old English word 'fabrile', meaning belonging to the craft, or 'hand-made'. The first year's production had gone straight into museums and it was not until 1896 that the first Favrile glass was offered for public sale. Favrile glass exploited the use of chemical soaks or vapours

Right: Three examples of Lava glass. Molten glass spilt over a rough surface produces the volcanic effect.

Below: One of the popular Jack-in-the-Pulpit vases which Tiffany made with numerous colour effects.

tion not produced when the glass was semi-molten. Millefiori Glass was a type of glass that had been known since the 2nd century BC, but the process was not revived until the 19th century. The decoration is composed of coloured glass rods which contain a motif, usually a flower, which passes through its entire length.

The various techniques and the range of shapes that he devised meant that no two pieces of Favrile glass are exactly the same. There are elegant flower forms and 'Goose-necked' vases inspired by Persian perfume flasks; 'Jack-in-the Pulpit' vases with bulb shaped bases and long slender bodies that flow into trumpet-shaped tops and the 'Tel el Amarna' vases, named after the excavation of Pharaoh Amenhotep IV's capital, which retain the simple shapes of their Egyptian models but with a more brilliant colour tone.

OFTEN IMITATED, NEVER BETTERED

There have been many imitators of Favrile glassware. In America, Frederick Carder who founded the Steuben Glassworks in Corning, New York, registered his iridescent glass as Steuben Glass and copied many of Tiffany's shapes. In Europe, many glassmakers came extremely close to reproducing Tiffany's style, including Loetz ,in Austria.. The Loetz glass, however had a very limited range of colours and never really achieved anything like the tactile quality of Tiffany Favrile glass.

Reinforced by commercial success, Tiffany spared no expense in his experiments and could afford to be ahead of his competitors. But it was not just his range of colours and extensive experimentation that gave Tiffany the edge over his contemporaries. His distinctive designs, with their fluid and sensual, organic movement, put him even further ahead.

Above: The famous Wisteria lamp, designed by Mrs Curtis Freshel,,was an enduring favourite from the Tiffany workshops.

Left: Tel el Armana vases in aquamarine blue retain the simple shapes of the original Egyptian models.

TIFFANY LAMPS

In 1900, Tiffany changed the name of his company to Tiffany Studios, the name it retained until its closure in 1938. Tiffany Studios continued to produce interior designs, Favrile glass, stained glass windows and mosaics, as well as numerous household goods including the most famous articles, the Tiffany lamps.

The lamps were a natural outlet for Tiffany's interest in glass and the effects of light on colour. He considered the harsh brightness of electricity and softened its glare with lovely colour. His designs were also technically considered: the electric lamps were given armatures to alter the focus of the light and shade could be interchangeable. In his lamps, Tiffany combined function with aesthetic appeal.

CANDACE WHEELER

Tiffany had started to sell lamps in 1895 although he had exhibited them earlier in the Women's Building at the World's Fair in 1893 in Chicago. Tiffany's former colleague Candace Wheeler was President of the Women's Building and from this association he recognised the talent of many women designers, a number of whom were to emerge from his studios. In the area of lamp design, Tiffany's two major designers were Mrs. Curtis Freschel and Clara Driscoll.

Freschel designed the famous Wisteria Lamp and Driscoll developed patterns for the Ivy, Rose, Geranium and Butterfly lamps, among numerous others. While the leaded glass shades were not an innovation from the Tiffany Studio,, the designs were nevertheless, far superior to any other similar products. Tiffany

Left: Leaves and fruit tumble over the shade of the Grapevine lamp.Note the textured base.

Left: The Ward Willits House, Highland Park, Illinois, designed by Frank Lloyd Wright. Stained glass was used in the windows to create coloured light effects inside.

lamps are often thought of in terms of their glass, but the stands and bases were integral to the design and under Tiffany's guidance, these too became works of art.

Byzantine designs were sometimes used and an antique appearance given to them by the use of dark, mossy colours which complemented the organic shapes of nature – leaves, tendrils, cobwebs, stems of flowers and roots of trees – that became the models for curving, sculptural forms. The leaded glass shades assumed the natural forms of branches and fruit and flowers or the circular spread of wings and spider's webs. Their titles confirm their origin and form: Pansy, Orange Petal, Snail, Queen Anne's Lace. All were realised in the jewel-like colours of Tiffany's stained glass.

Pattern moulds were made so that the same lamps could be reproduced again and again and made in various sizes. So widely popular did this style become in the United States that a 'Tiffany lamp' is now the generic term for any lamp with a stained glass shade.

FOLLOWING THE LEADER

The popularity of Tiffany glass obviously encouraged many other manufacturers to follow his lead. In 1893 Handel and Co. of Connecticut began producing cheaper versions of the Tiffany lamp and two former employees of the Tiffany Studio started the Quezal Art Glass and Decorating Company of Brooklyn in 1901. Other companies included the Fostoria Glass Speciality Company and Imperial Glass Company of Ohio, Fenton Art Glass Company of Virginia, Lustre Art Glass Co. of New York and Vineland Flint Glassworks of New Jersey. The latter produced a much debased version of Tiffany Favrile glass called Carnival glass, a pressed glass with a sprayed-on iridescence of rather vulgar orange tones.

A NEW GENIUS: FRANK LLOYD WRIGHT

While Tiffany was the undoubted master of glass, another towering figure in the history of American design, and arguably the greatest influence on design in the United States in the first half of the 20th century, is Frank Lloyd Wright.

Born in 1867 – just 19 years after Louis Comfort Tiffany – Wright was to create a style that still seems fresh and relevant today. Best known as the architect of his Prairie and Usonian houses, Wright's architectural designs reflected a variety of influences that were frequently underlined in the decorative accessories that he designed to complete the interiors and complement the buildings.

Not content to simply design an attractive

Above: Interior of Unity Church, Oak Park, Illinois by Frank Lloyd Wright, 1906.

Right: A collection of Tiffany iridescent glass vases, c.1900.

building, Wright also often designed the furnishings including light fixtures and art glass windows and screens. In 1894 Wright entered a competition to design an office building for the Luxfer Prism Company in Chicago, and instead of plate glass windows more typically used in commercial buildings, Wright incorporated the company's own glass blocks. Although not constructed, Wright's design made greater use of glass within its structural grid than any previous building, thus emphasising the geometry of the iron skeleton frame. In 1897 Wright patented a series of glass blocks for Luxfer, the design of which incorporated a stylised flower of circles and squares. The fluid lines of the design recall not only the influence of Wright's mentor, Louis Sullivan, but reflect the principles of English designers like Christopher Dresser and Owen Jones.

In his decorative schemes Wright also used leaded glass, often made by the Linden Glass Company of Chicago. Plain glass in totally geometric designs echoed the central motifs used within specific houses. The repeated scheme of flowers and leaves – often of sumac, a plant native to the Prairies – is evident in the 'Tree of Life' windows for the remarkable Darwin D. Martin House, and in the art glass designed for the Ward Willits House, the Dana-Thomas House, the Hollyhock House and the magnificent Robie House.

NON-OBJECTIVE, GEOMETRIC DESIGNS

In the Avery Coonley Playhouse, the two-dimensional abstract designs of the art glass windows were based on Wright's observation of a parade with balloons, flags and confetti-motifs that were most suitable for a kindergarten theatre. These windows, possibly Wright's greatest achievement in glass, were also some of his first non-objective, geometric designs.

ART NOUVEAU
CERAMICS

The ceramicists of the late 19th century remained, to a certain extent, outside the mainstream of decorative arts at the time, largely because of geography. In France, for example, the two main centres for Art Nouveau – except for ceramics – were Paris and Nancy, and although they participated in international exhibitions and at Paris Salons, French ceramicists were scattered around the country, using local clays, throwing, turning, glazing and firing their works in an isolated manner that demonstrated their profound love of their craft.

ART POTTERY

Many of the famous names in other fields of Art Nouveau design - Guimard, known for his ironwork for the Paris Métro, Gallé, best known for his work in glass, and de Feure and Colonna, best known as furniture designers – worked in ceramics as well. Often their work was more closely linked with the major porcelain factories: Guimard's ceramic designs were well suited to Sèvres porcelain. Rather than focusing on the natural warmth, texture and colour identifiable with stoneware, they were essentially hard-lined, abstract linear creations carried into three dimensions, in which the rising curve of the vase's silhouette is incorporated into the composition. George de Feure and Edward Colonna both designed for Limoges, an appropriate combination since both were sophisticated designers well-versed in 18th century style.

Overleaf:Vase by Taxile Doat, probably made before his departure for America.

Left: Glazed stoneware and pewter jug from Germany, dated 1606.

TRADITIONAL STONEWARE

Many among the new generation of craftsmen however, turned their backs on fine porcelain almost entirely, concentrating instead on the production of more coarsely grained, traditional stoneware which was the subject of an enormous revival in the Art Nouveau period.

Almost universally referred to as Art Pottery, the revival of stoneware created

Left: A tea bowl of low fired Raku ware with black glaze from Japan, 17th century. Such pieces have had a powerful effect on European studio potters.

throughout Europe and America, a whole new or revitalised tradition quite separate from that of porcelain production, and one that still thrives today.

'HONEST' MATERIALS

The choice of such a 'democratic' medium was influenced by the socially-conscious side of the Arts and Crafts Movement that preferred plainer, cheaper, 'honest' materials that were free from association with wealth and social aspirations. While the exploitation of stoneware had begun before the emergence of the Art Nouveau style, it was primarily those artists who were working in the Art Nouveau idiom that were responsible for developing the full potential of the medium. In Art Nouveau design, the increased range of materials and the exploration of materials

hitherto considered as 'inferior', places the emphasis on the aesthetic qualities of a piece rather than on the economic criteria.

ORIENTAL INFLUENCES

It is arguable whether the revival of stoneware would have been so significant if it had not been for the example of oriental, in particular Japanese, ceramics. Japanese wares, including pieces decorated with cloisonné (a type of enamelling), ivories and bronzes, were shown at the Paris Exhibition of 1862, and the revelation of their simple shapes, sparse decoration and asymmetrically placed motifs made a dramatic impact on those who saw them. The Frenchman Félix Bracquemond (1833-1914) produced possibly the best of the European japonaiserie in ceramics. Inspired by the discovery of a volume of sketches by

the artist Katsushika Hokusai, he made a series of woodcuts that were copied on to an earthenware service produced in 1866 by the firm of F.E Rousseau.

Chinese porcelain had already had a major impact on the west from the 18th century onwards. Among 19th century aesthetes such as James McNeill Whistler and Oscar Wilde, there was a great enthusiasm for blue-and-white porcelain, although working craftsmen were more excited by the technical possibilities of oriental stoneware. Warm, rich colours were as possible as glowing lustres. The chance effects of slip and glazes could be explored alongside a range of surface textures.

FRENCH CERAMICS

In addition to oriental models, advanced technical equipment and knowledge in Europe

Below: Three Chinese blue and white vases dated c.1640 (left) and 1662-1722 (middle and right).

helped Art Nouveau designers to create new artistic effects in ceramics. Supporting the works of the pioneering French ceramicists, in 1881 the Haviland workshop moved from Auteuil to Paris where it was managed by Ernest Chaplet. Here, Chaplet re-discovered

the technique for producing the much envied *sang-de-boeuf* (oxblood) glaze of Chinese stoneware, which was, as its name implies, deep red in colour. The secret of the process Chaplet never divulged, but versions were developed by contemporaries such as Adrien-

Pierre Dalpayrat, the inventor of a similar, copper based 'rouge Dalpayrat'. Dalpayrat is best known for his stoneware vases, sculpted either in strange twisted shapes, or in the form of animals, fruit or vegetables.

CHAPLET AND HAVILAND'S

In 1885 Chaplet bought the firm from Haviland's and together with Edouard and Albert Dammouse, Ringel d'Illzach, Hexamer and many others, Chaplet made dark red-brown stoneware with incised decoration, the coloured glazes encircled with gold in the manner of cloisonné enamels. It was at this time that the painter Paul Gauguin started experimenting with ceramics which were fired by Chaplet. Gauguin produced works which were free from the conventions of a specialist. His lack of inhibition in handling the clay resulted in primitive vessels of swelling and flowing forms many with gnarled and twisted handles. These works, which were few in number, were produced in the late 1880s, both before and after Gauguin's trip to Martinique and predate the development of the Art Nouveau proper of the 1890s.

PÂTE-SUR-PÂTE

Dammouse, who trained as a sculpture before devoting himself to ceramics, began his career by decorating in *pâte-sur-pâte* (paste on paste) in which decorations were build up in low relief with layers of porcelain slip. The varying thicknesses give the effect of shading in the design. When Chaplet sold Haviland on to Auguste Delahérche, Dammouse set up his own studio in the village of Sèvres where he made stoneware, faience and porcelain or-

Right: Stoneware vase by Adrien-Pierre Dalpayrat with ormolu mounts by Keller.

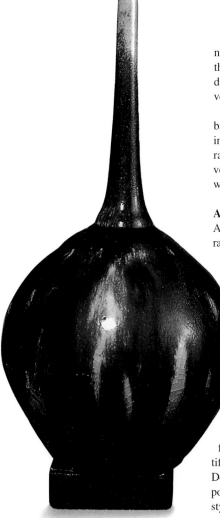

namented with flowers, leaves or seaweed. He then turned to making vases and bowls in a distinctive translucent paste of his own invention, and which were first exhibited in 1898.

Chaplet's decision to sell Haviland was based on his desire to continue his research into flambé glazes. The remarkable results ranged from the shiny *sang-de-boeuf* to veined, spotted and pitted turquoise and white.

AUGUSTE DELAHÉRCHE

Auguste Delahérche was a more prolific ceramicist than Chaplet. Between 1883 and 1886 he worked in saltglaze stoneware, but his aim to sell art ceramics at low prices met with little success. He began to use drip glazes which he had seen on Japanese stoneware, with engraved or raised floral decoration, which won him a gold medal at the 1889 Universal Exhibition in Paris. In 1894 Delahérche began a ten year period of experimentation in deep, pure monochromatic glazes on simple forms. After 1904, he made unique pieces, only keeping those which were perfect and refusing to accept any result, however beautiful, that was accidental. At the age of 68, Delahérche began to make delicate white porcelain vases with a pierced decoration of stylised flowers, now very rare.

CARRIÈS AND THE SCHOOL OF SAINT-ARMAND

A second centre for the production of stoneware was in the Nivernais region at the School of Saint-Armand-en-Puisaye. The leader here was the charismatic but short-lived figure Jean Carriès, who died aged 39. Out of his hands grew grotesque masks, goblins and fanciful animals. These bizarre creations are

Above: A hard-paste vase (1885-1904) by Ernst Chaplet, inspired by oriental sang-de-boeuf.

Right: A stoneware dish by Ernst Chaplet.

Far right: A stoneware vase by Albert Dammouse, c. 1900..

Right: Auguste Delahérche vase with blue drip glaze and peacock feather motif.

Far right: A selection of pierced stoneware vases by Auguste Delahérche.

some of the best examples of the fanciful and almost surreal side to much of the Art Nouveau borrowings from nature. All his work was left to his great friend Georges Hoentschel, a celebrated decorator, who also began to make stoneware for himself. Closer to the Japanese originals than Carriès, vases in sober blue, green, grey and beige were sometimes finished with ivory stoppers, and others were sometimes mounted in ormolu.

CERAMIC SCULPTURE AND ARCHITECTURE

Art Nouveau ceramic production was not simply limited to vases and bowls, but extended to the production of editions of sculptures. The application of stoneware to architecture was an important feature of the style. The leading figures in this field were Alexander Bigot, Emile Muller and Edmond Lachenal.

From 1894 Bigot produced plates with newts, frogs and mermaids in low relief swimming among deep translucent glazes, but from 1900, he turned towards making stoneware for both inside and outside buildings, among them Guimard's Castel Béranger, as well as editing sculptures.

IVRY

Muller's factory at Ivry produced stoneware sculptures and he was responsible for the edition of the well-known portrait of Yvette Guilbert by Toulouse-Lautrec. Muller, together with the firms of Gentil et Bourdet and Hyppolyte Boulanger, made much of the architectural ceramics of the time. Lachenal was a painter, sculptor and decorator whose stoneware vases ornamented with flowers and animals had a certain success, but he became particularly well known for his stoneware editions of Art Nouveau sculptures by Rodin, de Frumerie, Dejean, Fiz-Masseau and Saint-Marceaux.

Above: A gourd-shaped vase by Jean Carries exploiting poured glazes and enamel rich in oriental colours.

BRITAIN

The three principle influences in the applied arts in Britain in the second half of the 19th century were Gothicism, japonisme and Islamic art, and British ceramics of the late 19th century show these three very strongly. The willowy 'whiplash' curves of French Art Nouveau had a minor effect.

The 1870s had seen the foundation of a number of art-potteries which attempted to produce ceramics based on new ideas in design outside of the industrial factories. Of these the most important were Minton's Art Pottery Studio in London, the De Morgan Pottery, the Doulton factory of Lambeth, London and the Linthorpe Pottery of Middlesbrough in Yorkshire founded by John Harrison and Christopher Dresser in 1879.

SALTGLAZE

Doulton was concerned principally with the revival of medieval saltglaze stoneware, but also produced painted wears called Impasto and Faience, the latter based on the poster art of Alphonse Mucha. It was this type of pottery that was also the main product of Minton's Art Pottery Studio.

One of the most important British designers of the period was Christopher Dresser who began his career as a botanist before designing wallpaper, furniture, textiles, metalwork, glassware and ceramics for a number of companies. At the Linthorpe Factory most of Dresser's ceramic pieces in a dark, green-brown streaky abstract glazes, were influenced by his extensive knowledge of Japanese ceramics, while his monochrome yellow, green or blue wares were influenced by Chinese examples which Dresser also designed for Ault in the 1890s.

Art pottery was perhaps the area of design

where Arts and Crafts ideals were most widespread. Practically and financially, art pottery was – and is - a form where the artist-designer and craftsman could be one, and it is interesting to note that in America, many art potteries were established either for therapeutic purposes, or to provide a useful. but suitably lady-like occupation for women.

CERAMICS IN AMERICA

The initial impetus for American pottery came with the Philadelphia Centennial Exposition of 1876 where the first Oriental exhibits could be seen alongside works from the Doulton factory and Ernest Chaplet. Both the Robertson family from the Chelsea Keramic Art Works, and Mary Louise McLaughlin visited the ex-

Below: Stoneware vases and pears by Georges Hoentschel, Emile Grittel and Henri de Vallombreuse, c.1900.

hibition of ceramics and returned to their home states of Massachusetts and Ohio to put what they had seen into practice.

The development of American ceramics ran parallel to experimentation with the use of exotic glazes on simple stoneware shapes that occurred in France. The Roberstons specialised in Greek terracotta forms at first, but by 1877 had introduced their Chelsea faience, using simple shapes and soft colours. Around the

Above: A ceramic bust by Gustave Obiols. The dreamy maiden returns, this time in clay.

Left: Stoneware bust, 'Flore', by Louis Challon and Emile Muller, c. 1901.

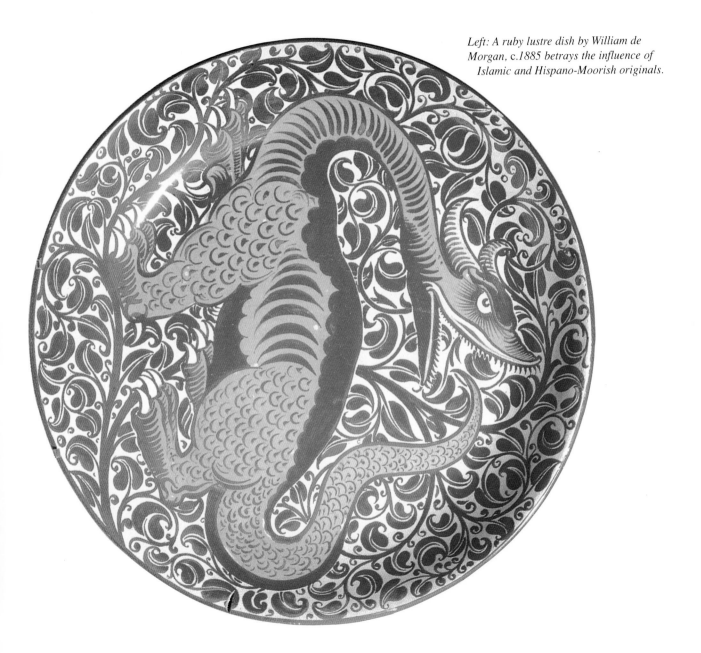

Left: A ruby lustre dish by William de Morgan, c.1885 betrays the influence of Islamic and Hispano-Moorish originals.

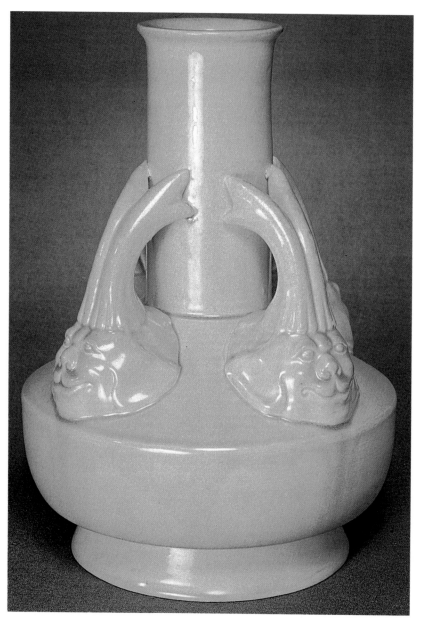

same time the process known as barbotine, painting with coloured slips, usually on a blue or green ground was introduced. Further experiments resulted in an American version of *sang-de-boeuf,* but also in financial trouble. The Chelsea works closed, but were re-opened in 1895 along more commercial lines as the Dedham Pottery, best known for its crackleware with blue-in glaze borders decorated with flowers and animals.

UNDERGLAZE

In Cincinnati, McLaughlin, an amateur enthusiast and another exponent of the underglaze technique, developed her Limoges glaze, which become known as Cincinnati Limoges. In 1879 she founded the Cincinnati Pottery Club to encourage other women in the craft. From 1881, the club used the firing facilities at the Rookwood Pottery, one of the most famous of the 30 or so potteries in Ohio. Rookwood was started by Maria Longwoth Nichols Storer with support from the ladies at the Cincinnati Pottery Club, and from 1880 to 1884 the output at Rookwood mainly consisted of the ladies' experiments, usually with much gilding and heavy relief or incised decoration. After this Rookwood was reorganised on a more commercial footing, but always maintained the tradition of allowing individual artists a free hand in their designs.

Rookwood ceramics were often characterised by underglazing, a difficult technique requiring mild firing to maintain the warm coloured glaze. When the pottery won a Grand Prix at the 1900 Paris Exhibition, a craze started for its elegant wares. Best known perhaps

Left: Grotesque vase designed by Christopher Dresser for William Ault, c. 1892.

are the vases, decorated with floral themes, animals and flowers – especially orchids and lilies - where the Art Nouveau style was seen to some degree in the elegant, elongated vase forms and curving plant-like handles.

DOAT

One of the most remarkable examples of the ascendancy of American pottery was the University City Pottery in Missouri. The pottery belonged to the Art Institute of the People's University started by the entrepreneur Edward Garner Lewis. Lewis was himself interested in ceramics and self-taught using a translation of French ceramicist Taxile Doat's *Grand Feu Ceramics* a treatise on new techniques in firing and glazing.

Doat was a ceramicist who made his name working in Sèvres, while at the same time, maintaining an independent production. Doat treated porcelain to the techniques of the stoneware innovators using dripped glazes and even the vegetable shapes of gourds, pumpkins and pears which had also been used by Carriès at Saint-Armand. Doat also varied the texture of his works by having pâte-sur-pâte medallions, like ancient cameos, applied to the surface, which proved to be popular.

Offered an extremely fine porcelain clay that had been found in the area, Doat was lured from his native Sèvres- along with his ceramics collection- by Lewis to University City in 1909 where he stayed for some five years giving Missouri stoneware an international reputation.

Although more usually associated with glass, Louis Comfort Tiffany began experimenting with pottery in 1898 at his Corona works in New York but from its inception, Tiffany's pottery was overshadowed by his Favrile glass and none of his ceramic wares were offered for public sale until 1905. The

Left: Blue and white serving bowl by Dedham Pottery who were best known for their animal and floral border patterns.

Below: A Rookwood Pottery tile, c.1911, features a pair of rabbits flanking a tulip tree.

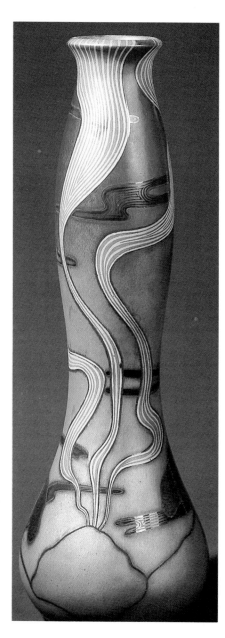

Left: A stoneware vase by Joseph Rippl-Ronai for Zsolnay of Hungary. The Hungarians introduced a distinctly central European element to forms and colour.

Below: A Rookwood Pottery vase, exhibited at the Paris Exposition Universelle in 1900.

pottery bases for his famous lamps were in fact purchased from the Greuby Pottery.

EASTERN EUROPE

Throughout the whole of Europe, ceramics followed much the same pattern as in most other countries. There were studio potters experimenting with new techniques, many small art potteries, as well as some fine work produced by some of the large established firms such as Meissen and Berlin in Germany, Joseph Bock in Vienna, the Rozenburg pottery in The Hague, and the two great Swedish factories, Rorstrand and Gustavberg.

An outstanding example of Hungarian Art Nouveau ceramic production is Zsolnay Pottery. Founded in 1862 by Vilmos Zsolnay at Pêcs, in its early days it produced earthenware in a semi-industrial, semi-folk style. In 1893 Vinsce Wartha was appointed artistic director and it was he who developed with Zsolnay the famous iridescent lustre glaze called Eosin.

Stylistically, Zsolnay's products can be divided into six groups: those in a traditional style; those in Lustre resembling Tiffany or Loetz glass; the figures; the dishes painted with flowers and landscapes in red, green and blue; the pots with animals sculpted in high relief and the pieces made early in the 20th century which show the influence of the Vienna Secession. In artistic terms, the designer Joszef Rippl-Ronai marks the high point in the factory's history for his flowing floral patterns and designs are most evidently Art Nouveau.